I0409666

Congressional
Research
Service

Consumers and Food Price Inflation

Randy Schnepf

Specialist in Agricultural Policy

October 4, 2012

Congressional Research Service

7-5700

www.crs.gov

R40545

CRS Report for Congress
Prepared for Members and Committees of Congress

Summary

Record Midwest heat in June and July (2012) sparked the worst U.S. drought since 1956, causing damage to major field crops. This situation has contributed to record U.S. prices for corn and soybeans in both cash and futures markets in 2012, and has fanned the fears of food price inflation reminiscent of 2008. The heightened commodity price volatility of 2008 and the subsequent acceleration in U.S. food price inflation associated with commodity market shifts raised concerns and generated many questions about farm and food price movements by Members of Congress and their constituents. However, historical evidence suggests that retail prices for processed food products are driven more by consumer demand (strongly linked to general economic conditions), than by price changes in raw commodity markets, although this linkage varies with the degree of raw commodity content in the retail product. For a discussion of the relationship between farm and retail prices, and the major factors influencing retail food prices, see CRS Report R40621, *Farm-to-Food Price Dynamics*, by Randy Schnepf. This report focuses instead on the nature and measurement of retail food price inflation and its relationship to consumers.

During the 1991 to 2006 period, U.S. food prices were fairly stable—annual food price inflation, as measured by the Consumer Price Index (CPI) for all food (excluding alcoholic beverages), averaged a relatively low 2.5%. However, several economic factors emerged in late 2005 that began to gradually push market prices higher for both raw agricultural commodities and energy costs, and ultimately retail food prices. U.S. food price inflation increased at a rate of 4% in 2007 and at 5.5% in 2008—the highest since 1990 and well above the general inflation rate of 3.8%. The situation of sharply rising prices came to a sudden halt in late 2008 when the financial crisis hit U.S. markets leading to a severe economic recession. Annual food price inflation dropped to 1.8% in 2009 and 0.8% in 2010, before rising to 3.7% in 2011 driven by improving U.S. and global economic conditions. USDA projects that annual food price inflation will range from 2.5% to 3.5% in 2012 and rise to 3%-4% in 2013.

The All-Food CPI has two components—food-at-home and food-away-from-home. The food-at-home CPI is most representative of retail food prices and is significantly more volatile than the food-away-from-home index. The food-at-home CPI is projected in a range of 3% to 4% for 2013, compared with a 2.5% to 3.5% annual inflation rate for food-away-from home prices. This difference is partially explained by the larger share of farm products in the final price of retail foods than in food-away-from home. Farm product prices are, in general, substantially more volatile than the other marketing and processing costs that enter into retail or ready-to-eat foods.

Many wages and salaries, as well as federal programs (including several domestic food assistance programs), are linked to price inflation through escalation clauses in order to retain consumer purchasing power. For households where income and federal benefits do not keep up with price inflation, declines in purchasing power are real and immediate. However, even for households with escalation clauses, a time lag usually occurs between the time the price inflation is measured and the time when the wage or program benefit is adjusted upward to compensate. The 2008-2009 global economic crisis—which involved higher retail prices and unemployment, income loss, and lower effective household purchasing power—resulted in higher participation rates in the federal food and nutrition programs since then. As a result, USDA's food and nutrition assistance programs have seen a tremendous expansion in use—federal expenditures totaled $103.3 billion in FY2011 and marked the 11th consecutive year in which food and nutrition assistance expenditures exceeded the previous historical record. Since FY2000, expenditures for food and nutrition assistance have more than tripled.

Contents

Figures

Tables

Contacts

Introduction

Everyone eats. As a result, everyone is affected to some degree by food price changes. This makes understanding food price changes and their effects on consumers an important matter for Congress. This report provides information on the current status and outlook for U.S. food prices, measuring their changes and how such changes relate to U.S. consumers.

The first section of the report, "Consumer Demand," briefly reviews the major economic concepts underlying consumer food behavior. The second section, the "Consumer Price Index," describes how U.S. food price inflation rates have evolved since 1915, when federal price data collection for inflation-measuring purposes began. The third section, "Consumer Income and Expenditures," provides information on recent history and projections for U.S. food expenditure shares relative to total household budget, with comparisons across income quintiles, as well as internationally. The fourth section, "Recent Food Price Inflation," examines retail food price inflation, including a review and discussion of the level of food price inflation registered by the consumer price index for all-food, at-home, and away-from-home food purchases as well as for major food groups. Finally, a fifth section, entitled "Effect of High Prices," discusses the impact that rapid food price inflation can have on government food programs and the more vulnerable consumer groups.

Each section may be read independently of the others. Thus, those readers that are concerned primarily with the status of U.S. food price inflation may proceed directly to the sections entitled "Historic Price Inflation Patterns," Recent Food Price Inflation" or "Effect of High Prices."

Consumer Demand

Consumer demand is influenced by economic factors—own-price, the price of close substitutes, the price of complementary items, and household income—as well as by several non-economic factors including tastes and preferences, family size, age of family members, geographic location, shopping behavior, and lifestyle choices. Economists attempt to study and measure the nature of consumer behavior in response to changes in prices, incomes, and household characteristics, with an eye for understanding the potential social welfare outcomes that may result from price and income changes across different socioeconomic groups. Policymakers, in turn, often attempt to use that information to design and implement policies that mitigate the more deleterious effects of price and income changes on consumers.

Price Responsiveness

In general, consumers will use less of any good if its price increases relative to other goods (referred to as the pure "substitution effect" by economists). However, a consumer's price responsiveness is a matter of degree and is subject to the potential influence of disposable income as well as other non-price factors such as those listed in the preceding paragraph.

Under most circumstances, the availability of many close substitutes is likely to make consumers more sensitive or responsive to price changes, because they have the opportunity to switch to similar alternatives. In contrast, a lack of substitutes may give the consumer little choice but to continue to purchase the available good, even as its price rises, especially if it is deemed a necessity. Strong ethnic or cultural tastes and preferences may endear a person to a particular food type such that he or she will continue to purchase that food as its price rises even in the presence of abundant substitutes (for example, ethnic groups that are accustomed to eating rice at every meal may be reluctant to switch to bread or potatoes even if the price of rice rises relative to those other foods).

Rapid or unexpected changes in retail food prices will impact some consumers more than others depending on income levels and the importance of the affected food items in consumers' budgets. In general, if an item represents a very small portion of the consumer's budget (for example, consider salt), then a consumer is less likely to respond to a price change. Basic food staples such as bread, potatoes, pasta, and rice tend to take smaller shares of the consumer's food budget (relative to meat, dairy products, fruits and vegetables, and more processed food products) and, as a result, consumers are less responsive to a change in their price. In contrast, high-valued food items such as expensive cuts of meat or seafood probably represent more costly (and infrequently purchased) delicacies for most households. As a result, most households will tend to be far more responsive to changes in the prices of such high-valued products than for basic staples. Often a price change for an item within a specific food group[1] may result in consumers switching to lower-quality items within that food category—the classic example being a switch from steak to hamburger when meat prices rise. In contrast, a widespread price rise across all food groups may engender substantial reshuffling of consumer food budget allocations as households try to meet their nutritional goals with their limited budgets.

Of course, the absolute size of a consumer's disposable income is also important in determining actual purchasing power. For households with smaller incomes, the food budget itself is likely a larger portion of total household expenditures, and such households are likely to be more responsive to price changes across all food categories than are higher-income households.

In summary, lower-income consumers who spend a significant share of their household budget on food are likely to be impacted more severely by rising food prices (and are likely to be more responsive to price changes) than high-income consumers with lower food budget shares.

Income Responsiveness

A household's absolute level of disposable income (and, to a lesser degree, wealth) directly affects its ability to respond to price changes. As a result, as household incomes grow, consumers often opt for more expensive or higher-quality selections of foods than are presently in their food budget, or may experiment by trying new or unfamiliar foods. For example, as incomes increase in less-developed countries, it is common to see per-capita expenditures on meat and dairy products increase. In contrast, when incomes decline, consumers tend to pull back from more expensive options. If the income decline is severe and is perceived as permanent or long-lasting, consumers may make substantial changes to their food budget choices.

In the aggregate, household consumption behavior in response to perceived income changes (if persistent and widespread) may affect a country's agricultural production or trade patterns, or it

---

[1] Examples of food groups include meat, dairy products, bakery goods, fruits, or vegetables.

may impact the health and nutritional status of certain segments of the population. As a result, it is important for policymakers to monitor household wealth and income levels and distribution for unexpected shifts that may have important economic or health consequences.

Economists call the relationship between changes in consumer income and the quantity of an item purchased an *Engel curve*. This relationship is used by economists to classify goods.

- For a **normal good**, consumers buy more of it as their incomes increase, but at a decreasing rate such that its average budget share declines for higher income levels.

- For a **luxury good**, consumers buy more of it as their incomes increase and at an increasing rate such that its budget share increases at higher income levels.

- For an **inferior good**, consumers buy less of it as their incomes increase.

Of course, different goods will be classified differently by different people since tastes and preferences also are important. However, with respect to the overall food budget, in the aggregate certain behavioral norms are expected. *Engel's law* is the idea (largely validated by data with some minor exceptions) that food, in general, is a normal good, so that the budget share spent on food declines as a consumer's income rises. While Engel's law is generally observable for individual households, it tends to hold best in the aggregate—that is, when considering an entire population. To the extent that this "law" holds, then the proportion of a nation's income spent on food serves as a good index for international comparisons of relative consumer welfare (**Table 3**).

Tastes and Preferences

Non-economic factors such as cultural or ethnic preferences may determine both the share of a particular food product in the household's budget (e.g., rice represents a larger share of per-capita expenditure in most Asian households than in most European households at similar income levels) as well as a household's responsiveness to a change in the price of a particular product.

Dietary needs also change with age. For example, young children and adolescents generally need both more calories and a higher portion of protein-based calories to meet nutritional demands of rapid physical growth and high activity levels. Populations or households with a large share of individuals from this demographic stratum are more likely to consume larger per-capita portions of meat and dairy products than an older, more mature and sedentary population would. As a result, population demographics such as household composition, size, and age structure often play an important role in consumer price sensitivity and income responsiveness. In increasingly affluent societies, lifestyle choices, when complemented with sufficient purchasing power, can also play an influential role in household food purchases.

Summary

For households with low disposable income levels where food expenditures are a large share of the budget, rising food prices result in greater responsiveness and may force more difficult budgetary tradeoffs than in higher-income households with smaller food-budget shares. Of course the opposite effect is true during periods of falling prices. However, each household's price and income effects also are influenced by its particular set of non-economic characteristics.

The Consumer Price Index (CPI)

The CPI is perhaps the most widely reported measure of U.S. price inflation.[2] The CPI is used both as an economic indicator of retail price inflation and as a means of adjusting current-period values for inflation. The "All-Items" CPI is the index most often referred to (i.e., the headline CPI) for representing consumer price inflation. It is generally divided into eight major spending categories, including a "Food and Beverage" category comprising 15.3% of the overall index. The CPI category of "Food and Beverages" is composed of two major subcategories: "All-Food" (which has a relative weight of 14.3% in the all-items CPI), and "Alcoholic Beverages" (1.0%).

Figure I. CPI Weights for Major Categories

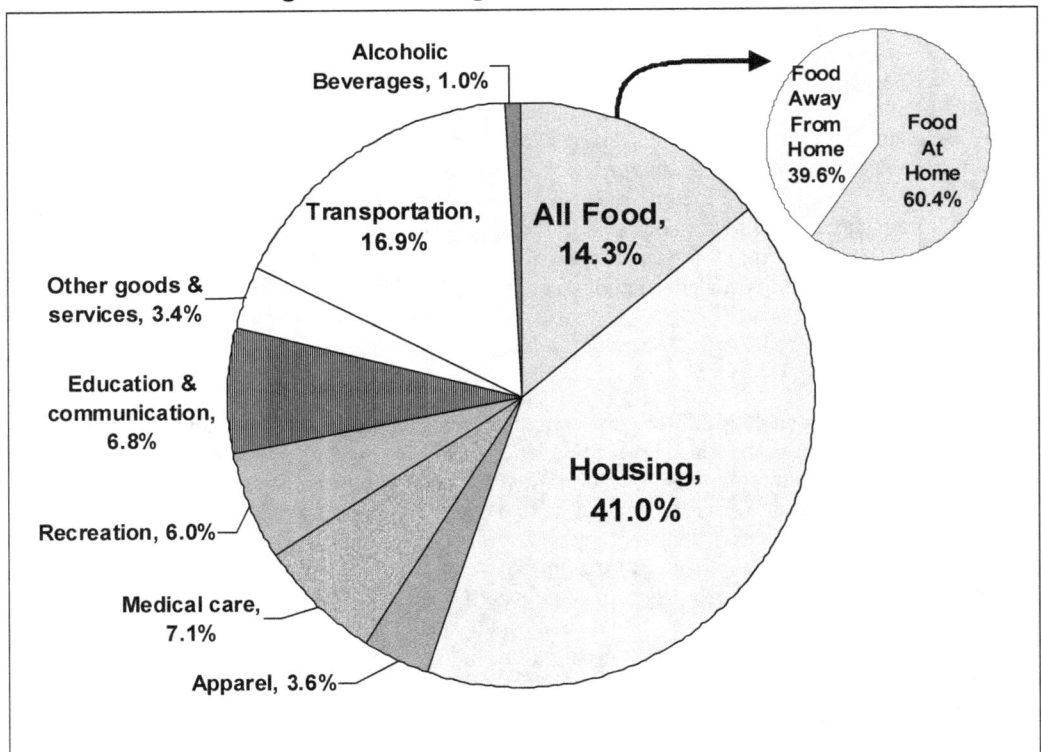

Source: Bureau of Labor Statistics (BLS), U.S. Dept. of Labor, CPI-U, 2009-10 weights, December 2011

The All-Food CPI is the principal indicator of consumer food price changes (**Figure 1**). The All-Food CPI can be subdivided into the "Food-at-Home" (60.4%) and "Food-Away-from-Home" (39.6%) categories. The **Food-At-Home CPI** reflects changes in the prices of foods consumed at home. As such it is the principal indicator of changes in retail food prices in the United States. The **Food-Away-From-Home CPI** reflects changes in the prices of foods purchased outside of

---

[2] See CRS Report RL30074, *The Consumer Price Index: A Brief Overview*, by Brian W. Cashell.

the home, primarily at eating and drinking places such as restaurants and other eating establishments. However, it also includes price changes for ready-to-eat foods purchased at hotels and motels, recreational places and sporting events, vending machines, and school and work cafeterias.

Historic Price Inflation Patterns

Over time, the All-Food and All-Items CPIs have moved together, although the All-Food CPI has been consistently more variable than the All-Items CPI (**Table 1** and **Figure 2**). Prior to 1960, both of these indexes exhibited higher average inflation rates and more volatility than in recent years. During the 1914-1920 period, both price indexes recorded double-digit annual inflation. Food inflation hit its all-time high of 28.7% in 1917 (**Figure 2**). All-Items price inflation peaked a year later at 18%. Just four years later retail prices entered a prolonged deflationary period, starting in 1921 with a deflationary plunge of -24.2% for All-Food and -10.5% for All-Items, that lasted until 1941 when war time shortages finally renewed retail price inflation.

Table 1. Retail Price Change, Mean and Variability, by Historic Time Period

(all data—mean and standard deviation (SD)—are percentages)

CPI Series	1914-1920		1921-1941		1941-1960		1960-1983		1983-2011	
	Mean	SD	Mean	SD	Mean	SD	Mean	SD	Mean	SD
All-Items	10.8	7.4	-1.4	4.5	3.9	4.1	5.3	3.6	3.0	1.1
Energy	—	—	—	—	—	—	6.9	9.1	3.5	8.3
All-Food	11.6	9.6	-1.8	9.0	4.9	7.2	5.2	4.1	3.0	1.3
At-Home	—	—	—	—	—	—	5.0	4.5	2.9	1.7
Away-from-Home	—	—	—	—	—	—	6.0	3.1	3.1	1.0
Core[a]	—	—	—	—	—	—	5.1	3.3	3.0	1.2

Source: Calculations were made by CRS based on BLS CPI data.

Notes: "—" = not available. The mean is the average annual price change for each period. The standard deviation (SD) is a measure of dispersion around the mean value for each period. Plus or minus one (two) SD captures 68.2% (95.4%) of the variation around the mean value for each period. The mean and SD have been calculated using the annual percent change data for each of the five different periods. A larger SD implies greater variability, for example, all-food price inflation has shown a clear pattern of declining variability as the SD has fallen from 9.6% during the 1914-20 period to 4.1% during 1960-83 (more than halving the variability), and finally to 1.3% during 1983-2011. This decline in variability is clearly evident in **Figure 2**.

a. The "Core" price index is the all-items CPI without the energy and all-food components.

The variability of the overall CPI and its individual components is important because uncertainty about price changes makes planning more difficult—whether the meal planning of a household, the investment planning of a business, or the policy intervention planning of a federal agency.

During the 1941-1960 period, price inflation remained extremely volatile, alternating between spikes of inflation and steep disinflationary (i.e., deflationary) drops. It was not until 1960 that retail prices stabilized with tolerably mild inflation. However, this proved short-lived as the 1970s saw a return to sharp price spikes generated by an energy crisis and rapid, unexpected shifts in global crop supply and demand.[3] By the early 1980s, retail price inflation had returned to modest levels below 5%. Since 1983 retail prices, as measured by the all-items and the all-food CPIs, have been relatively low and relatively stable, except for temporary surges in 1989-1990 and again in 2007-2008.

Figure 2. Annual Price Inflation, 1915-2013: All-Items vs. All-Food

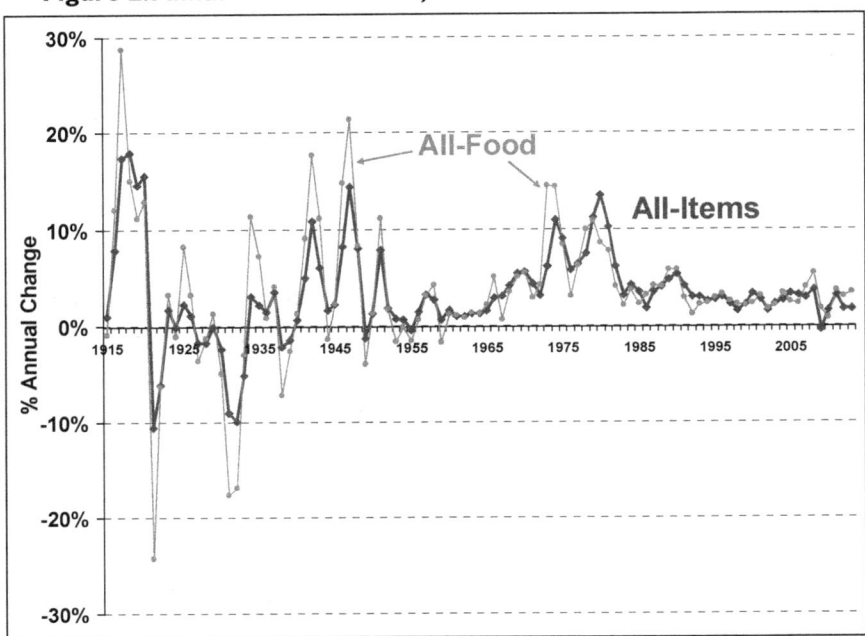

Source: Department of Labor, Bureau of Labor Statistics, 1915 through 2011. The CPI values for 2012 and 2013 are forecast by Global Insights (All-Items) and USDA's Economic Research Service (All-Food).

Notes: The percent change is calculated from the annual average CPI for successive years.

Overall Inflation versus Core Inflation

Many economists and policymakers believe that the food and energy components of the CPI are volatile and subject to shocks not easily dealt with through government monetary policy. In response, the BLS also reports another price index, referred to as the "core" index because it removes the food and energy price components from the all-items CPI.[4] The so-called core CPI is thought to be a useful measure of underlying trend inflation in the short run. According to BLS

---

[3] For a discussion of 1970s energy markets, see CRS Report R40187, *U.S. Energy: Overview and Key Statistics*, by Carl E. Behrens and Carol Glover. For a discussion of 1970s agricultural markets, see M. Peters, S. Langley, and P. Westcott, "Agricultural Commodity Price Spikes in the 1970s and 1990s," *Amber Waves*, ERS, USDA, March 2009, at http://www.ers.usda.gov/; and P. Riley, "Global Grain Markets in 1996: Shades of 1972-74?" *Agricultural Outlook*, AO-233, ERS, USDA, Sept. 1996, pp. 2-6.

[4] For more information, see CRS Report RS22705, *Inflation: Core vs. Headline*, by Marc Labonte.

data, the food component of the CPI, although more volatile than the overall CPI, is still substantially less volatile than the energy component (**Figure 3** and **Table 1**).

Figure 3. Annual Price Inflation Since 1960: All-Items, All-Food, and Energy

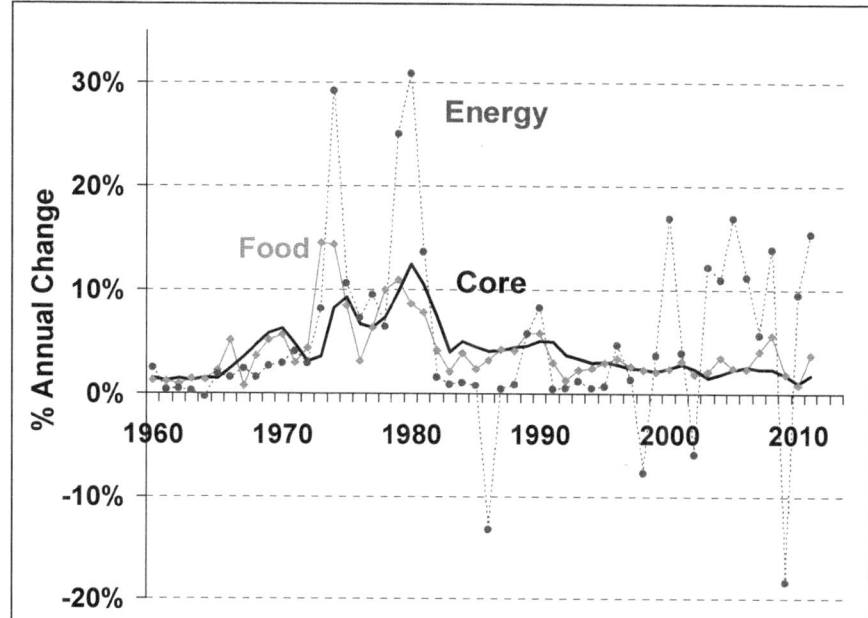

Source: Department of Labor, Bureau of Labor Statistics.

Since 1960, the energy price index has been a more volatile component of the All-Items CPI than the food price index by a substantial margin. For example, the energy price inflation standard deviation (SD) of 9.1% was more than double the All-Food SD of 4.1% during the 1960-1983 period, and nearly six times larger since 1983 (8.3% versus 1.3%).

Since 1983 both the All-Food and the All-Items CPIs have been lower (in terms of average values) and substantially more stable (in terms of SDs) than during the preceding seven decades. In contrast, the energy price index has remained nearly as volatile since 1983 (although at a lower mean level) as it was during the preceding two decades. This is an important point because the energy price index has seen its weighted share of the CPI gradually increase over time and, although energy's current weight share of 9.7% is slightly more than half that of the food weight share of 15.3%, energy price inflation is far more insidious than food inflation to the extent that energy costs figure in the retail price of practically every other component of the CPI.

Consumer Income and Expenditures

A household allocates its available income across a range of expenditure, savings, and investment choices. As mentioned earlier, food expenditures as a share of a household's total budget are an indicator of sensitivity (or vulnerability) to unexpected food price changes. At the national level, food budget share (via Engel's law) can be used as a general indicator of welfare among nations.

Food as a Share of Consumer's Budget

According to Bureau of Economic Analysis (BEA) estimates, in 2010 total U.S. disposable personal income (DPI) was $11,127 billion, or $35,920 per capita.[5] ERS calculates that, on average, 9.4% of disposable personal income was spent on food.[6]

Figure 4 shows the evolution of the average food budget share against U.S. DPI per capita in constant 1982-1984 average dollars. By both measures (food budget share and real DPI per capita), U.S. consumers have seen their "well-being" improve substantially over the past 70 years. (Note that these are national averages that ignore any potential distribution issues.) The U.S. food share of real DPI has fallen from a high of 25.2% in 1933 to under 10% since 2000, while the average DPI per capita (in 1982-1984 dollars) has risen from $3,629 in 1933 to over $16,000 by 2006.

Figure 4. Comparison of Real U.S. Disposable Personal Income (DPI) Per Capita and the Share of DPI Spent on Food, 1930-2010

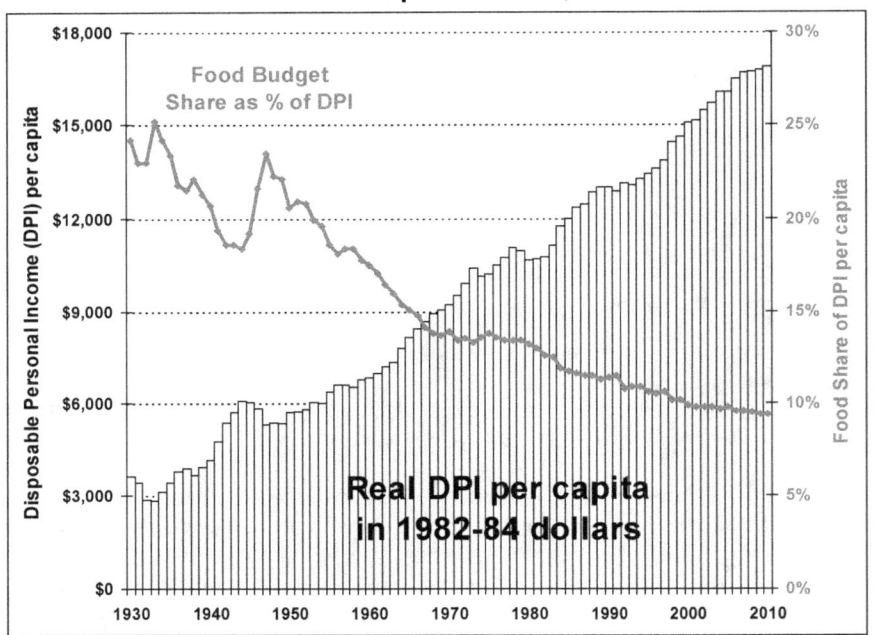

Source: "Food CPI, Prices and Expenditures Briefing Room," Food Expenditure Tables, ERS, USDA.

Notes: Real DPI is BEA nominal DPI series deflated by the all-items CPI with base 1982-1984 = 100; real food expenditures are the ERS series of food expenditures deflated by the all-food CPI with base 1982-1984 = 100.

---

[5] "Table 2.1. Personal Income and Its Disposition," National Income and Product Accounts, September 27, 2012, BEA, U.S. Dept. of Commerce. Estimates for 2011 total and per-capita DPI were $11,549 billion and $37,012, respectively. Comparable food expenditure data for 2011 were not available as of September 2012.

[6] The DPI and DPI-food-share estimates are for 2010 from Table 7, Food Expenditure Tables, *Food CPI, Prices and Expenditures* Briefing Room, ERS, USDA, at http://www.ers.usda.gov/Briefing/CPIFoodAndExpenditures/Data/.

When measured as a share of average total consumer expenditures of $49,705 per household (based on Consumer Expenditure Survey (CES) data, **Table 2**), average food outlays of $6,458 per household accounted for 13.0% of total spending in 2011.[7] Note that the difference between the two estimates of food budget share (9.4% based on DPI versus 13.0% based on CES total expenditures) is due to how disposable income and food expenditures are calculated for each of these indicators.

Table 2. Average Household Food Expenditures in 2011 by Income Quintiles

Income Quintile	Total	All Food		Food-at-Home		Food-Away-from-Home	
Expenditures (and Share of Expenditures) per Household							
Lowest 20%	$22,001	$3,547	16.1%	$2,448	11.1%	$1,099	5.0%
Second 20%	$32,092	$4,659	14.5%	$3,051	9.5%	$1,608	5.0%
Third 20%	$42,403	$5,620	13.3%	$3,496	8.2%	$2,125	5.0%
Fourth 20%	$57,460	$7,466	13.0%	$4,364	7.6%	$3,103	5.4%
Highest 20%	$94,551	$10,991	11.6%	$5,828	6.2%	$5,163	5.5%
Average Outlay ($)	**$49,705**	**$6,458**	**13.0%**	**$3,838**	**7.7%**	**$2,620**	**5.3%**
Share of Food Expenditures							
Lowest 20%		100%		69.0%		31.0%	
Second 20%		100%		65.5%		34.5%	
Third 20%		100%		62.2%		37.8%	
Fourth 20%		100%		58.5%		41.6%	
Highest 20%		100%		53.0%		47.0%	
Average Outlay ($)		**100%**		**59.4%**		**40.6%**	

Source: Table 1. Quintiles of before-tax income: Average annual expenditures and characteristics, Consumer Expenditure Survey, 2011, BLS, Dept. of Labor, at http://www.bls.gov/cex/2011/Standard/quintile.pdf.

The estimated food share of household expenditures (**Table 2**) varied across income quintiles in the United States, in accordance with Engel's law—that is, each succeeding higher income quintile increased its absolute expenditures on food (in dollar terms), but at a decreasing rate such that the food budget share declines across higher quintiles. For example, the lowest 20% of U.S. households spent $3,547 on food, or 16.1% of their average total expenditures of $22,001 in 2011. The budget food outlay increases in absolute dollars, while the food budget share declines across income quintiles until the wealthiest quintile, where households spent an average of $10,991 on food, or 11.6% of their total budget of $94,551.

Another clear pattern that emerges from the CES data (lower portion of **Table 2**) is the propensity to spend more of the food budget on away-from-home food consumption at higher income levels, both in absolute dollars and as a share of the food budget, thereby meeting the description of a

---

[7] CES data are calculated "per consumer unit" which is described as "similar to a household" by BLS.

luxury good. Or, otherwise stated, lower-income U.S. households tend to spend a larger share of their food budget on at-home consumption (69% in 2011) and are thus more vulnerable to unexpected retail food price increases (this is discussed further in the next section).

At-Home versus Away-from-Home Consumption

U.S. households have shown a strong propensity over time to increase their share of annual food consumption outside of the home (**Figure 5**). This tendency is associated with increasing per-capita disposable income as mentioned above. It is also associated with increasing female participation in the labor force, more two-earner households, increased advertising and promotion by large food-service chains, increasing time constraints on household members (e.g., longer commutes, increased work hours and less leisure time, etc.), the smaller size of U.S. households, and the increased availability of relatively low-cost fast food establishments.[8]

Figure 5. Average U.S. Food Expenditure Shares: At-Home vs. Away-from-Home

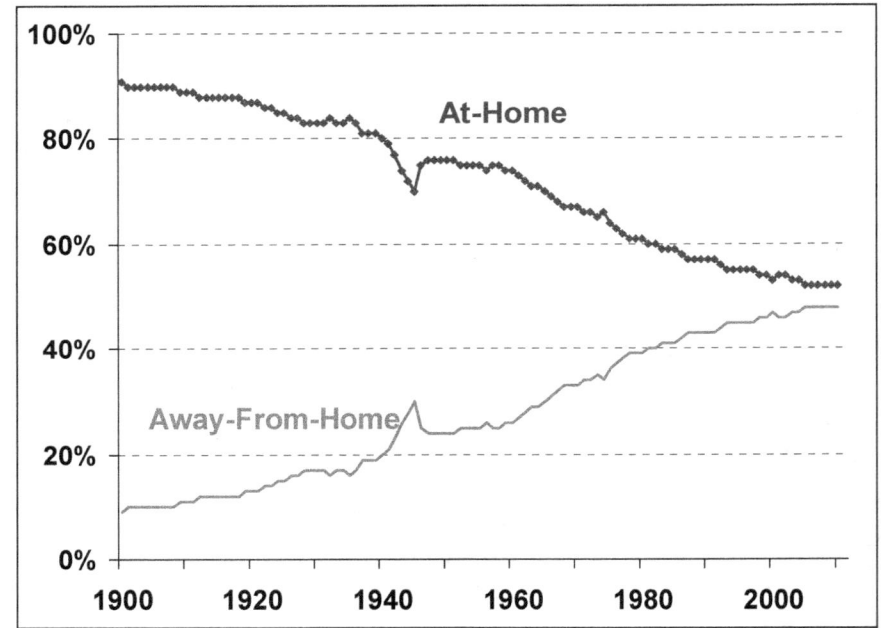

Source: Table 7, "Food CPI, Prices and Expenditures Briefing Room," Food Expenditure Tables, ERS, USDA, available at http://www.ers.usda.gov/Briefing/CPIFoodAndExpenditures/Data/.

With the exception of a brief period following the end of World War II, the portion of the national food budget spent on food consumption away from the home has steadily increased from 9% in

---

[8] For a discussion of this issue, see "Food Away From Home," *Diet Quality and Food Consumption* Briefing Room, ERS, USDA, at http://www.ers.usda.gov/Briefing/DietQuality/.

1900 to an estimated 48% in 2010. This phenomenon has important implications for consumer responsiveness to price and income changes, as well as for household nutrition.

The prices of food-at-home purchases are significantly more volatile than are prices of food-away-from-home purchases (**Table 1** and **Figure 6**). ERS research suggests that away-from-home expenditures are typically higher for single-person households and households containing multiple adults without living-at-home children.[9] By implication, households with living-at-home children typically rely more on at-home food consumption (as a share of their budget) and are thus more vulnerable to the normally higher price variability associated with retail food prices.

Figure 6. Monthly Food Price Inflation Since 2000: At-Home vs. Away-from-Home

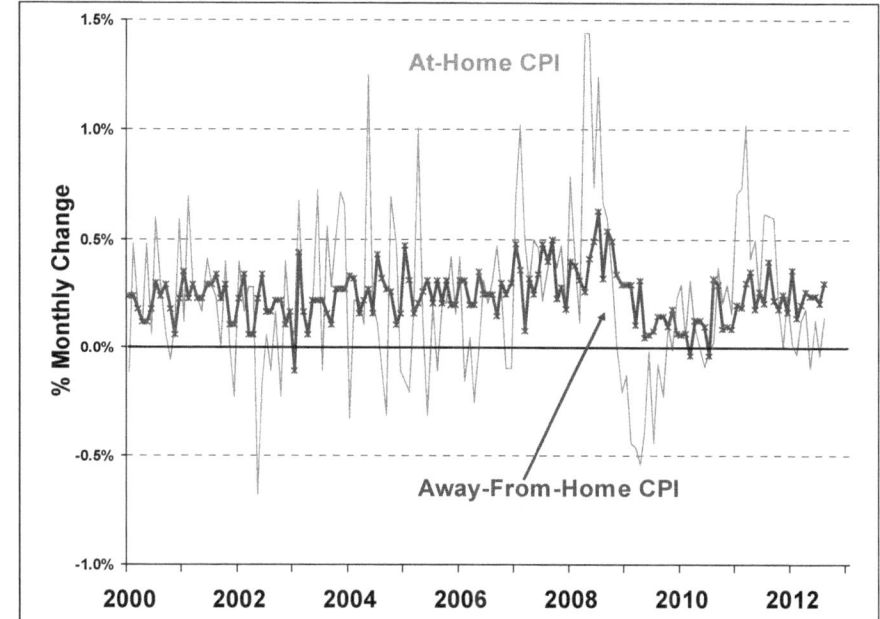

Source: BLS, U.S. Dept. of Labor.

Notes: Month-to-month inflation measured as the percent change in the monthly seasonally adjusted CPI for each index.

Although increased food-away-from-home expenditure is associated with higher income (both in absolute terms and as a share of the household food budget), it is not always a luxury item. A partial key to understanding how increasing food-away-from-home consumption may impact consumer behavior is the extent to which such consumption is a choice (for example, made in the evenings or on weekends during leisure hours) or more of an obligation (made during work hours), as well as the extent to which a consumer has alternative dining choices when eating out

---

[9] Hayden Stewart, Noel Blisard, Sanjib Bhuyan, and Rodolfo M. Nayga, Jr., *The Demand for Food Away From Home: Full-Service or Fast Food?* AER No. 829, ERS, January 2004.

(for example, subsidized cafeteria meals are often available at schools or in large institutional work settings).

International Comparisons

The Economic Research Service (ERS) includes in its food expenditure data series a comparison of food budget shares (based on at-home food expenditures) for over 70 countries. **Table 3** includes samples of countries from the ERS database ranked in terms of their at-home food expenditure budget shares, from smallest to largest. These data suggest that, on average, the United States has achieved a higher level of social welfare (based on this particular indicator) than any of the other countries in the database.

Table 3. International Comparison of Food-at-Home Budget Shares, Selected Countries, 2011

Country	Total Expenditures per capita	At-Home Food Expenditures per capita	At-Home Food Share
United States	$33,575	$2,239	6.7%
United Kingdom	$23,728	$2,225	9.4%
Canada	$27,632	$2,688	9.7%
Germany	$23,937	$2,658	11.1%
South Korea	$11,961	$1,506	12.6%
France	$24,576	$3,263	13.3%
Italy	$22,397	$3,276	14.6%
Japan	$27,143	$3,988	14.7%
Brazil	$7,573	$1,204	15.9%
Poland	$8,208	$1,648	20.1%
China	$2,134	$454	21.3%
Mexico	$6,819	$1,547	22.7%
India	$892	$235	26.3%
Russia	$6,400	$2,000	31.2%
Indonesia	$1,981	$631	31.9%
Philippines	$1,703	$614	36.1%
Nigeria	$765	$303	39.6%
Pakistan	$862	$359	41.7%
Egypt	$2,206	$963	43.6%
Algeria	$1,674	$732	43.7%

Source: Table 97, "Food CPI, Prices and Expenditures Briefing Room," Food Expenditure Tables, ERS, USDA, available at http://www.ers.usda.gov/data-products/food-expenditures.aspx/.

The food budget share is only one indicator of national welfare, and it ignores any unfavorable distribution of the food expenditure share (should any exist). Referring back to **Table 2** for the at-home food budget share for U.S. income and total expenditure quintiles based on CES data, it would appear that even the lowest 20% of U.S. households, on average, spend less than 12% of their budgets on at-home food consumption and thus appear relatively well-off in food terms based on this particular international standard. Readers should note that this cursory assessment is aggregate in nature and does not exclude the possibility that there are food-deficient individuals within the lowest 20% quintile of the U.S. population. According to ERS, in 2011, an estimated 14.9% of U.S. households were food-insecure at least some time during the course of the year— meaning that the food intake of one or more household members was reduced and their eating patterns were disrupted at times during the year because the household lacked money and other resources for food.[10]

Recent Food Price Inflation

This section provides a discussion of observed food price inflation in recent years based on CPI data. It is important to remember that the various CPI categories discussed here are indicative of price changes at the retail level in U.S. urban settings. As such, they are indicative of the prices faced by most consumers living in the United States (approximately 87% of U.S. consumers are covered by the CPI data collection process).

Annual All-Food versus All-Items Price Inflation

As a general rule, the all-item and all-food CPIs tend to move together. Following a relatively tumultuous period of price inflation in the late 1980s, both price indexes entered an extended period of relative stability. From 1991 through 2006, the all-food CPI measured average annual inflation of 2.5%, compared with 2.7% annual average all-items price inflation (**Figure 7**). However, several economic factors emerged in late 2005 that began to gradually push market prices higher for both raw agricultural commodities and energy costs.[11] These factors included the rapid development of the U.S. biofuels sector, as well as rising consumer incomes, not just in the United States but globally, which sparked demand for meat and dairy products, food and feed grains, and raw materials ranging from minerals and metals to coal and petroleum. In 2007, U.S. food price inflation reached 4% (**Figure 8**), the highest since 1990.

In early 2008, monthly food price inflation began to accelerate (**Figure 9**). In July 2008, the month-to-month food price change was 0.96% (equivalent to an annual rate of 12.1% if sustained for the entire year). Monthly retail food price inflation responds with a lag of several months to price changes in raw commodity markets. For the entire year, 2008 food prices rose by 5.5%, well above the all-items CPI of 3.8% (**Figure 7**).

---

[10] *Household Food Security in the United States in 2011*, Economic Research Report No. (ERR-141), by Alisha Coleman-Jensen, Mark Nord, Margaret Andrews, and Steven Carlson, 37 pp, September 2012, ERS, USDA, at http://www.ers.usda.gov/publications/err-economic-research-report/err141.aspx.

[11] For more information on the factors behind the sharp run-up in global commodity prices in the first half of 2008, see CRS Report RL34474, *High Agricultural Commodity Prices: What Are the Issues?* by Randy Schnepf.

Figure 7. Annual Price Inflation: All-Items vs. All-Food, 1985-2013F

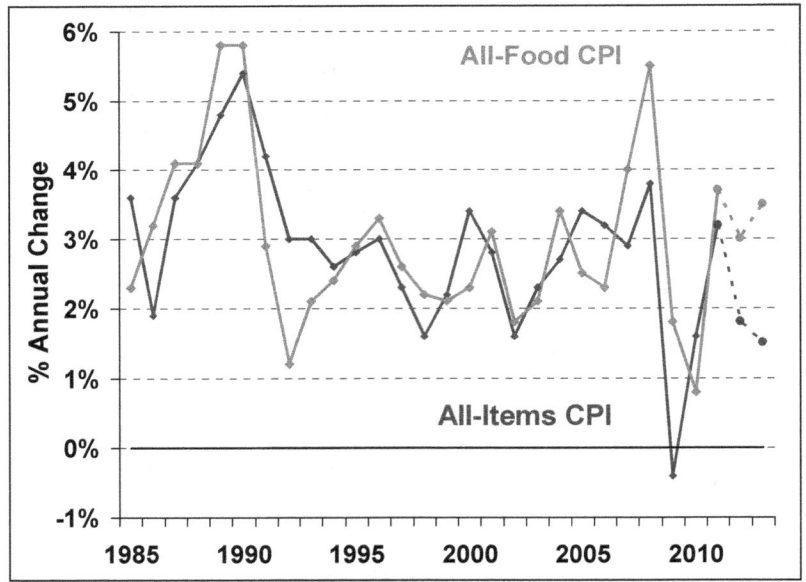

Source: Historical data, adjusted for seasonality, For 1985-2011, data are from the Dept. of Labor, BLS. Forecasts for 2012 and 2013 all-food CPI are from USDA, ERS, as of September 25, 2012; all-items CPI data for 2011 to 2013 are from Global Insights, U.S. Flash Forecast, September 2012.

Notes: The percent change is calculated from the annual average CPI for successive years.

Figure 8. Annual Food Price Inflation Since 1997

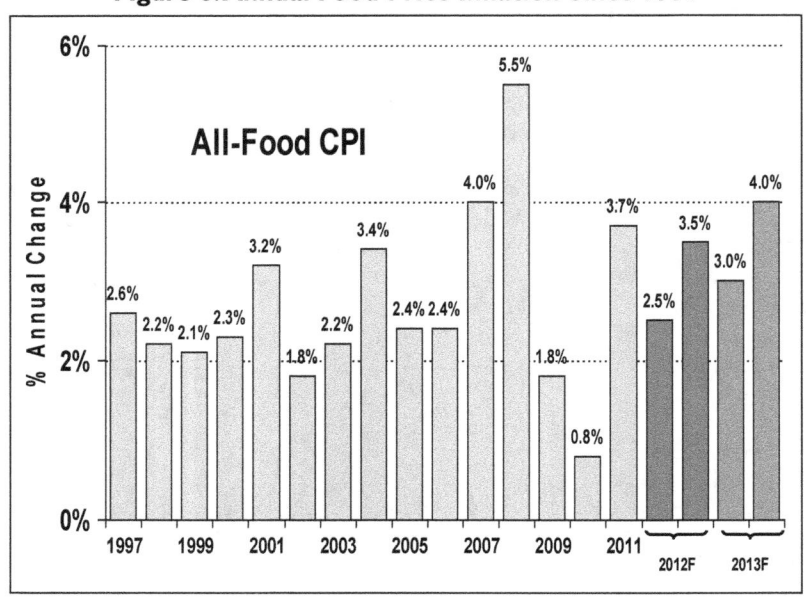

Source: Historical data (1985-2011) are from the Dept. of Labor, BLS. Forecasts for the 2012 and 2013 all-food CPI is from USDA, ERS, September, 2012.

The 2008 Financial Crisis Triggers a Severe Recession

The situation of sharply rising prices through the first half of 2008 came to a sudden halt in late 2008 when the financial crisis hit U.S. markets leading to a severe economic recession. Retail price trends reversed themselves and began following prices for raw agricultural commodities, which had already started to decline by late spring of 2008. Annual food price inflation dropped from 5.5% in 2008 to 1.8% in 2009. Although the downward monthly price inflation trend reversed itself in mid-2009, average annual food price inflation continued to fall, hitting 0.8% in 2010 (**Figure 8**).[12]

Sharply lower commodity and energy costs combined with weak domestic and global economies to reduce inflationary pressures from 2008 levels for both the All-Items and All-Food price indexes. However, the All-Items CPI was subject to much stronger deflationary pressures than the All-Food CPI. As a result, the disparity between the two indexes widened in 2009 as the All-Items CPI fell at an annual rate of -0.4% (**Figure 7**). By late 2009 global economies resumed growing, albeit slowly, followed in 2010 by a gradual return to growth in the U.S. economy, thus reversing the deflationary price pattern.

The 2012 and 2013 Forecasts for Annual Food Price Inflation

U.S. and global economies remain sluggish into late 2012 dampened by high unemployment, an on-going financial crisis in Europe, and a slowing economy in China. Despite this economic uncertainty, tight U.S. and global commodity market supply and demand conditions (due largely to poor growing conditions in the United States, Central Europe and elsewhere during 2012), are expected to keep food price inflation in the 3% to 4% range through 2013.

The Recent Monthly All-Food Price Inflation Pattern

When the all-food CPI is adjusted for seasonal variations and expressed on a monthly basis, a strong pattern of cyclical volatility can be seen to have emerged since January 2007 (**Figure 9**). First, was the highly volatile, upward pattern of price inflation during the first half of 2008. Second, the financial crisis struck and monthly price changes declined sharply. By November 2008 monthly retail food price inflation had fallen to near 0% (see **Figure 9**), then in December 2008 they actually fell below the preceding month's level (i.e., the monthly All-Food CPI deflated or become negative) for the first time since November 2006. Monthly food price changes continued their deflationary trend hitting bottom in May of 2009. Month-to-month retail food price declines continued into 2009 even though farm prices had stabilized in early 2009. This is because food processors and retailers are traditionally slow to pass on price decreases that they experience at the wholesale level for several reasons, including substantial inherent operating risk associated with volatile markets.[13]

---

[12] ERS updates its food price forecast monthly at *Food CPI and Expenditures* Briefing Room, ERS, USDA, at http://www.ers.usda.gov/data-products/food-price-outlook.aspx.

[13] These issues are discussed in more detail in CRS Report R40621, *Farm-to-Food Price Dynamics*, by Randy Schnepf.

Figure 9. Monthly Retail Food Price Inflation Spiked in 2008, Plummeted in 2009, Then Trended Up Into Early 2011, But Has Trended Lower Since

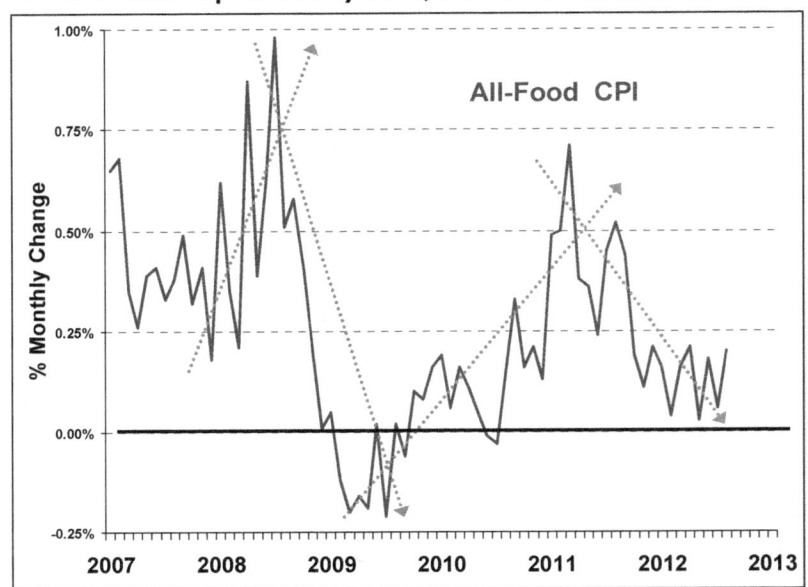

Source: Data, adjusted for seasonality, are from the Department of Labor, BLS.

Notes: The percent change is calculated from the CPI for successive months. Multiply any given month's value by 12 to approximate the annual inflation rate experienced during that particular month, without compounding.

Figure 10. Food Price Inflation Volatility Has Increased Since 2005

Monthly Change vs. 11-Mo. Moving Ave.

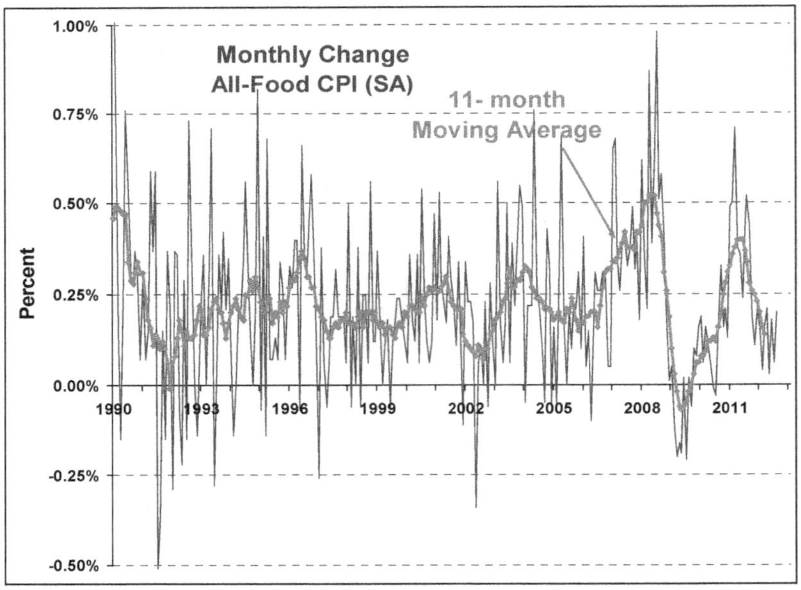

Source: Data, adjusted for seasonality, are from the Department of Labor, BLS.

Third, food prices began a jerky upward trend from May 2009 into early 2011 as both global and U.S. economic activity regains strength. Finally, after several months of revived economic growth and improving employment numbers in the United States, the economy slowed sharply again in early 2011. This economic turn-around was reflected in declining monthly price inflation data into 2012 (**Figure 9**).

Retail food prices were clearly responding to the on-again, off-again demand driven by the shifting of U.S. and global economic activity. The same monthly all-food price inflation measures (also adjusted for seasonality) are presented in **Figure 10**, but for a longer time period and accompanied by their 11-month moving average (MA).[14] The MA series reveals more clearly these same four inflationary trends for food prices: a strong upward inflationary trend that began at the end of 2005 and persisted through June 2008; a severe downward until mid-2009; another upward trend into early 2011, and finally, a decline in inflationary pressure into 2012 where monthly food price inflation appears to have leveled off.

At-Home versus Away-from-Home Food Price Inflation

As shown earlier (**Figure 6**), at-home food prices are substantially more volatile than away-from-home food prices (see also **Table 1**, where the at-home food price SD of 1.7% compares with a 1.0% SD for away-from-home food prices since 1983). This volatility is apparent, even when using a shorter time period (**Table 4** and **Figure 11**). It is not surprising, then, that at-home food prices made a steeper decline in 2009 and 2010, but a sharper reversal in 2011 than either all-food or food-away-from-home.

Table 4. Annual Food Price Inflation Since 2008

Category	Weights	2008	2009	2010	2011	2012F	2013F
All-Items	na	3.8	-0.4	1.6	3.2	2.0	1.4
All-Food	100%	5.5	1.8	0.8	3.7	2.5 to 3.5	3.0 to 4.0
Food-at-Home	60.4%	6.4	0.5	0.3	4.8	2.5 to 3.5	3.0 to 4.0
Food-Away-from-Home	39.6%	4.4	3.5	1.3	1.9	2.0 to 3.0	2.5 to 3.5

Source: Historical data (adjusted for seasonality) through 2011 are from BLS, Dept of Labor; 2012 and 2013 forecasts are from ERS, USDA, as of September 25, 2012. The all-items CPI forecasts for 2012 and 2013 are from Global Insights, U.S. Forecast Flash, September 2012.

Notes: BLS data are as of September 2012 using 2009-2010 weights (December 2011) for U.S. City Average (CPI-U). Annual percent changes are calculated from annual average indexes.

[14] Moving averages are used to reveal underlying patterns or trends that can otherwise be hidden by a substantial amount of month-to-month variation in price movements.

Figure 11. Annual Food Price Inflation for All, At-Home, and Away-from-Home CPI

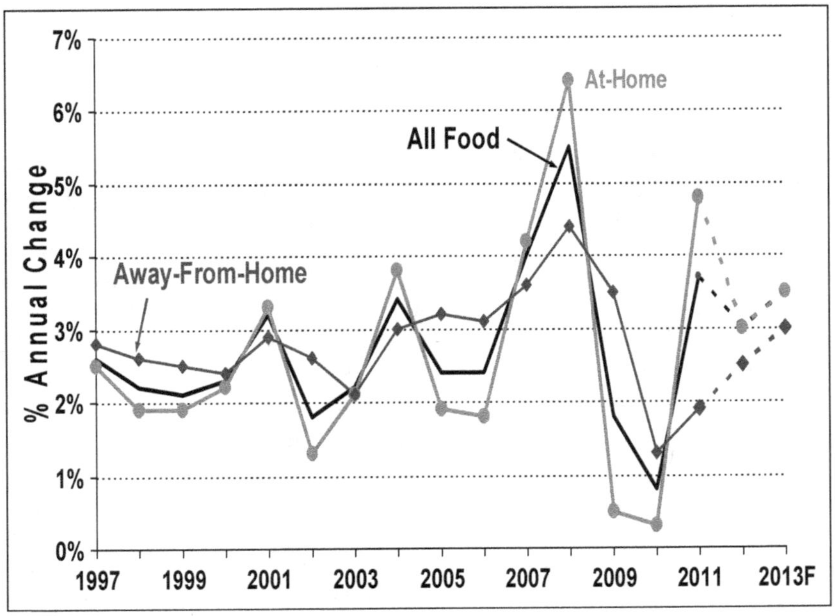

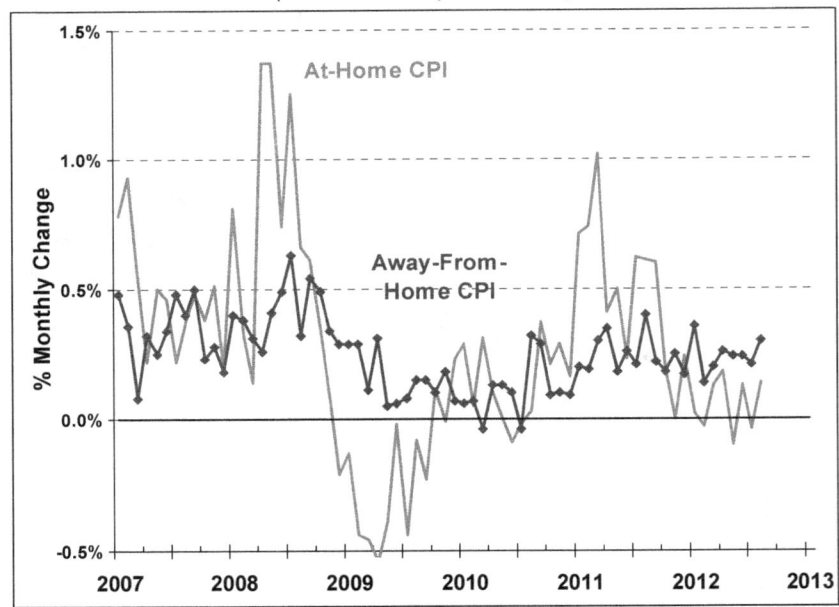

Source: See source info from **Table 4**.

Figure 12. Monthly Retail Food Price Inflation Since July 2007

(at-home vs. away-from-home)

Source: Historical data (adjusted for seasonality) are from BLS, Dept of Labor.

Notes: The percent change is calculated from the CPI for successive months. Multiply any given month's value by 12 to approximate the annual inflation rate experienced during that particular month, without compounding.

When displayed in terms of monthly price changes, the pattern exhibited by at-home food price inflation (**Figure 12**) appears very similar to the pattern for all-food price inflation (**Figure 9**), although the at-home food price movements are more extreme. In contrast, monthly away-from-home price inflation is much more stable. Note that both at-home and away-from-home monthly price inflation show a distinct downturn beginning in July 2008 and running into early 2009, followed by a steady recovery into 2011. However, the monthly away-from-home price inflation does not show the same declining trend that started in mid-2011 for at-home monthly price inflation.

Price Inflation by Major Food Categories

The demand-side influences of income growth (and decline) and the global financial crisis that emerged in late 2008 have already been discussed briefly. On the supply side, food price inflation is the result of dynamic forces that occur both at the farm where the raw agricultural ingredients for retail food items are produced, and along the marketing chain as the farm output is transformed and moved to the retail customer. An array of costs are layered on top of the price of the raw agricultural commodity, including handling, transportation, storage, and processing, as well as the insurance, financing, and advertising costs necessary to move the product to the retail customer. The relative importance of these marketing costs varies widely for different retail food products depending on the degree of processing and transformation (i.e., cleaning, packaging, shipping, advertising, etc.). As a result, economic forces such as higher energy costs or increased labor rates do not impact all food categories equally.

Annual Price Movements by Major Food Categories

The food price inflation is not felt evenly across all food groups, but varies widely in terms of both the timing and the relative magnitude of inflation. For example, in 2008, the inflation rate for at-home food was 6.4% (**Table 5**); however, only the "fruits and vegetables" category experienced a similar level of price inflation (6.2%). Several product categories experienced substantially higher inflation, including egg prices, which were up 14% in 2008 after having soared by 29% in 2007; fats and oils were up 13.8%, cereals and bakery products up 10.2%, snacks up 8.1%, and dairy products up 8%. In contrast, the broad price index of meats, poultry, and fish was up only 4.2%, and non-alcoholic beverages (including carbonated and non-carbonated drinks and juices) were up 4.3%.

In 2009 most food groups experienced reduced price inflation; however, several categories actually experienced price deflation—eggs (-14.7%), dairy and products (-6.4%), and fruits and vegetables (-2.1%). Similarly, the price inflation of 2010 and 2011 did not occur uniformly across all food categories. In fact, several food categories spiked sharply in 2010 before deflating in 2011. For example, cereal and bakery product prices rose 10.2% in 2010, but declined 0.8% in 2011; fats and oil prices rose 13.8% in 2010, but declined 0.3% in 2011; egg prices rose 14% in 2010, but only 1.5% in 2011; and dairy product prices rose 8% in 2010, but only 1.1% in 2011.

In 2012 and 2013, at-home food prices are forecast to rise within a range of 2.5% to 3.5% and 3.0% to 4.0%, respectively, with beef, poultry, cereal products, and fats and oils leading the way.

Table 5. The Food-at-Home CPI by Category Since 2008

Category	Weights[a] %	%	Annual Percent Change 2008	2009	2010	2011	2012F	2013F
Food at Home	**100%**		**6.4**	**0.5**	**0.3**	**4.8**	**2.5 to 3.5**	**3.0 to 4.0**
1-Cereal & Bakery Products	14.4%		10.2	3.2	10.2	-0.8	3.5 to 4.5	3.0 to 4.0
Cereals and products[b]		5.6%	10.1	3.4	10.1	-1.9	Na	Na
Bakery products[c]		8.8%	10.3	3.0	10.3	-0.4	Na	Na
2-Meats; Poultry; & Fish	22.7%		4.2	0.5	4.2	1.9	3.5 to 4.5	3.0 to 4.0
Beef & veal		6.3%	4.5	-1.0	4.5	2.9	3.5 to 4.5	4.0 to 5.0
Pork		4.4%	2.3	-2.0	2.3	4.7	1.0 to 2.0	2.5 to 3.5
Poultry		3.9%	5.0	1.7	5.0	-0.1	3.5 to 4.5	3.0 to 4.0
Fish & seafood		3.6%	6.0	3.6	6.0	1.1	3.0 to 4.0	2.5 to 3.5
3-Eggs	1.3%		14.0	-14.7	14.0	1.5	2.5 to 3.5	3.0 to 4.0
4-Dairy & Products	10.6%		8.0	-6.4	8.0	1.1	2.0 to 3.0	3.5 to 4.5
Milk		3.5%	6.0	-13.2	6.0	3.6	Na	Na
Cheese		3.4%	12.1	-5.2	12.1	0.7	Na	Na
Ice Cream		1.6%	5.1	2.0	5.1	-0.8	Na	Na
Other		2.2%	7.7	-2.4	7.7	-0.7	Na	Na
5-Fruits & Vegetables	14.9%		6.2	-2.1	6.2	0.2	0.0 to 1.0	2.0 to 3.0
Fresh fruits		5.9%	4.8	-6.1	4.8	-0.6	1.0 to 2.0	2.5 to 3.5
Fresh vegetables		5.5%	5.6	-3.4	5.6	2.0	-2.0 to-1.0	3.0 to 4.0
Processed fruits & veg.		3.5%	9.5	6.6	9.5	-1.3	3.0 to 4.0	2.0 to 3.0
6-Non-alcoholic Beverages	11.1%		4.3	1.9	4.3	-0.9	1.5 to 2.5	2.5 to 3.5
Juices & non-alc. drinks		8.3%	4.4	2.6	4.4	-1.4	Na	Na
Coffee, tea, & other		2.8%	4.2	0.4	4.2	0.6	Na	Na
7-Sugar & Sweets	3.6%		5.5	5.6	5.5	2.2	2.0 to 3.0	2.0 to 3.0
8-Fats & Oils	3.0%		13.8	2.3	13.8	-0.3	5.0 to 6.0	2.0 to 3.0
9-Other Foods[d]	19.7%		5.2	3.7	5.2	-0.5	3.0 to 4.0	3.5 to 4.5
Froz./freeze-dried foods		3.5%	4.3	2.8	4.3	-1.7	Na	Na
Snacks		3.7%	8.1	6.7	8.1	1.6	Na	Na

Source: Historical data (adjusted for seasonality) for 2008 to 2011 are from BLS, Department of Labor, for the U.S. City Average (CPI-U). The 2012 and 2013 forecasts are from ERS, USDA, as of September 25, 2012.

a. Weights are "as a percent of total at-home food expenditures" based on BLS 2009-10 weights, Dec. 2011.

b. Flour and prepared flour mixes, breakfast cereals, rice, pasta, and cornmeal.

c. Bread, fresh biscuits, rolls, muffins, cakes, cupcakes, cookies, and other bakery products.

d. Includes soups, spices, seasonings, condiments, sauces, baby food, and other miscellaneous foods.

Monthly Price Movements by Major Food Categories

Annual averages can cloud over substantial inter-year price movements. As a result, it is worthwhile to glance over the monthly price indexes for the past five years to get a better sense of the general pattern of retail food price movements across the various food groups. Monthly price indexes (**Figure 13**) for the four principal food groups—cereals and bakery products; meats (including beef, pork, poultry, and seafood); dairy products (including milk, cheese, ice cream, and other); and fruits and vegetables (including fresh as well as processed)—reveal very different patterns of price movement.[15]

Figure 13. Monthly Retail Price Indexes: Various Major Food Groups

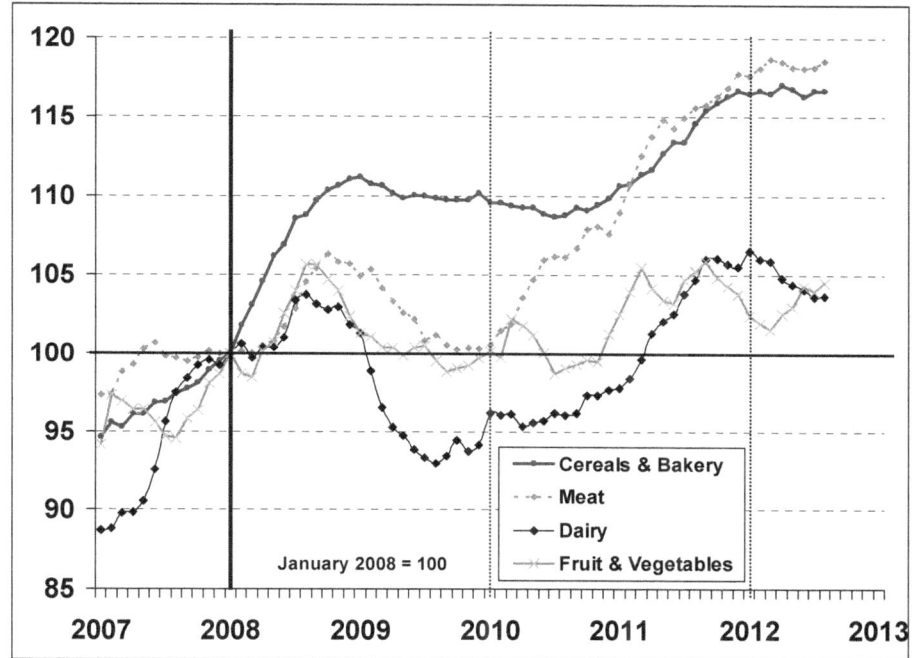

Source: Seasonally adjusted monthly CPI data, BLS, Department of Labor.

The cereals and bakery product price index and the meat price index show the strongest increase since 2008, rising nearly 19% and 17%, respectively, by 2012. The dairy price index rose through 2007 and into 2008, then declined sharply through 2009 before moving steadily upward from mid-2009 until 2012. The fruit and vegetable price index has shown considerable volatility, as a general upward pattern has been punctuated by significant deflationary movements during 2007, 2009, 2010, and late 2011.

---

[15] Note that these statistics (based on the change in monthly price indexes) differ from the statistics reported in **Table 5**, where the inflation rates are calculated using the difference from annual averages rather than monthly averages.

Perhaps the most dramatic and volatile of the individual foods price indexes has been eggs (**Figure 14**), which rose 35% from January 2007 to January 2008, then fell over 20% by July 2009. A year-over-year production decline from 2006 to 2007 coupled with strong exports tightened U.S. egg supplies and pushed prices sharply higher in 2007. Stronger egg production by mid-2008 coupled with the global economic crisis dampened prices starting in the later half of 2008. General economic growth has pulled egg prices upward steadily since mid-2009, but they have yet to return to their mid-2008 peak.

Figure 14. Monthly Retail Price Indexes: Beef, Pork, Poultry, and Eggs

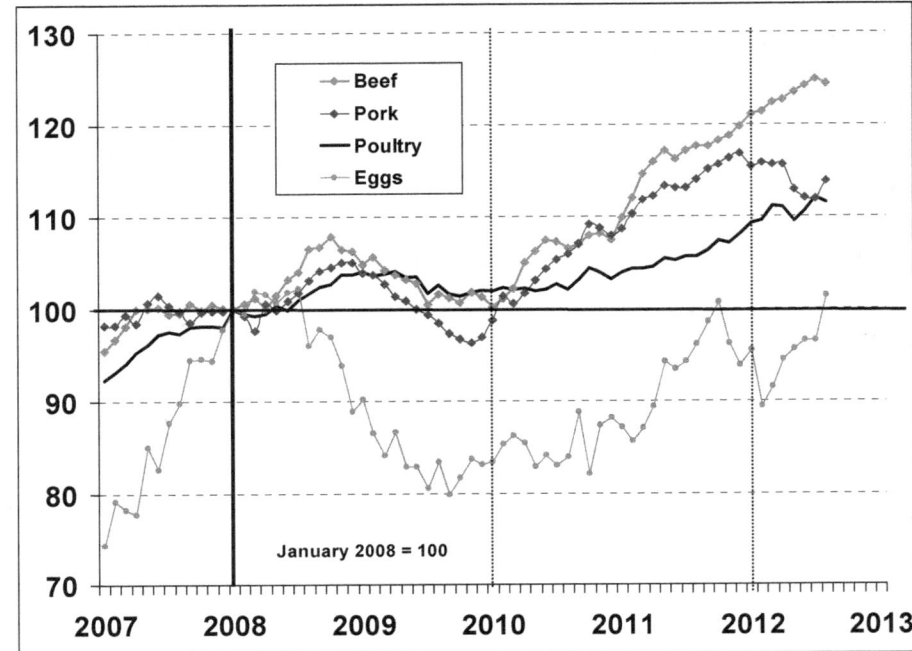

Source: Seasonally adjusted monthly CPI data, BLS, Department of Labor.

Beef and pork prices have shown considerable strength since early 2010 although pork prices have tailed off since late 2010. Drought-related declines in cattle populations are expected to support beef prices through 2013. Poultry prices have been more stable and have ticked upward since the last half of 2010.

The components of the dairy group (**Figure 15**) followed distinctly different patterns, particularly the price index for fresh milk, which showed a sharp escalation in early 2007 (up 20% on the year), followed by a sharp drop-off in 2008, including a 22% fall from July 2008 to August 2009, before trending higher. The milk price pattern for the 2007-2009 period was very similar to the egg price pattern for that period, and for the same principal reasons—initially tight supplies and expensive feed costs, followed by increased supplies and a sharp drop in demand. U.S. milk production expanded through 2007, while the global economic crisis weakened demand. A resumption of U.S. and global economic growth (albeit slow) has helped sustain price increases since late 2009; however, the dairy price index has yet to return to its 2008 level. In contrast, highly processed ice cream showed a fairly steady upward rise from mid-2007 before slowing in early 2009, then growing sharply in late 2010 with the improving general economy.

Figure 15. Monthly Retail Price Indexes: Dairy, Fresh Milk, Cheese, and Ice Cream

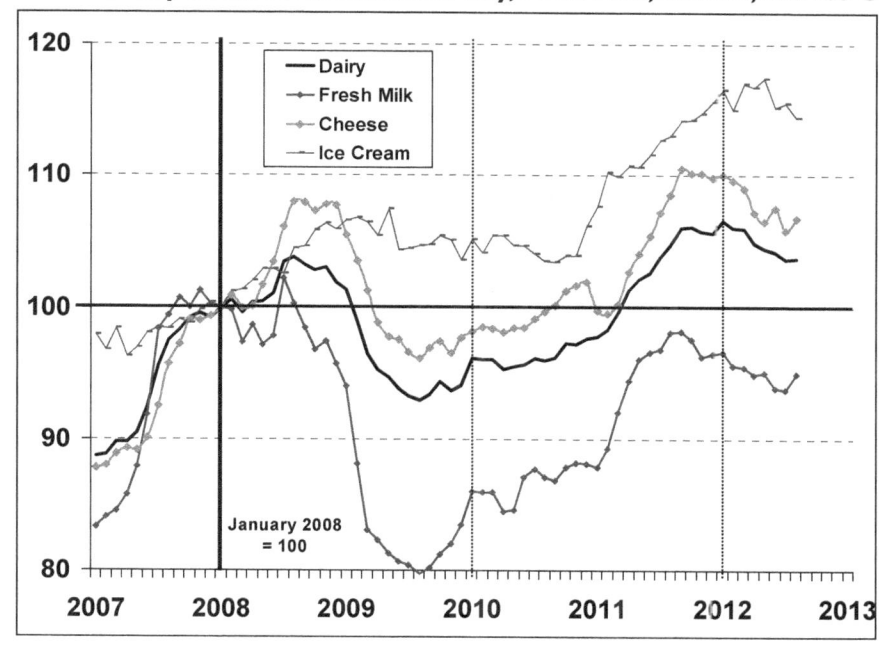

Source: Seasonally adjusted monthly CPI data, BLS, Department of Labor.

Figure 16. Monthly Retail Price Indexes: Fruits and Vegetables

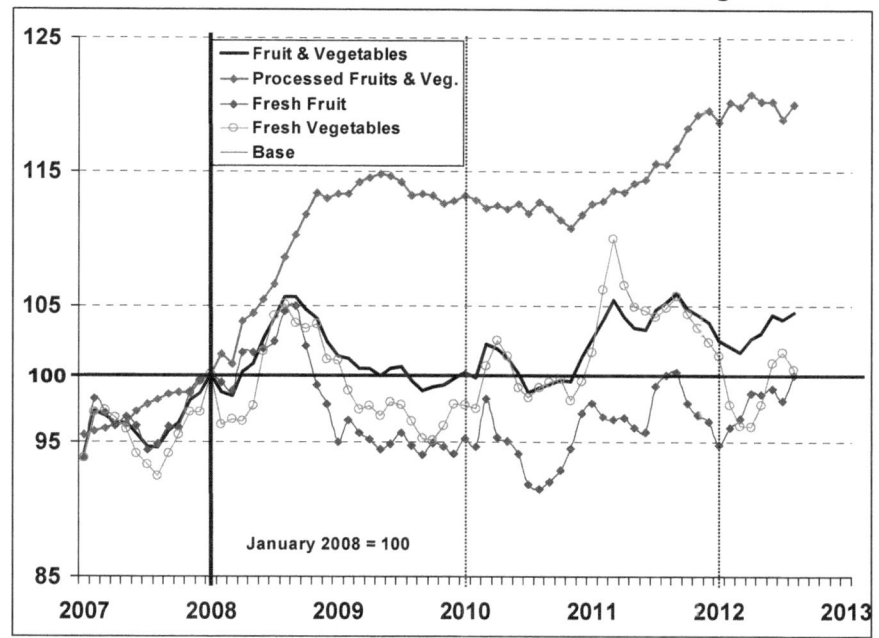

Source: Seasonally adjusted monthly CPI data, BLS, Department of Labor.

Similar to ice cream, the price index for processed fruits and vegetables (**Figure 16**) rose steadily through 2008, before leveling off, then ticking upward again since late 2010. In contrast, the price indexes for fresh fruit and fresh vegetables exhibited volatile, slightly upward patterns into mid-2008 before declining through mid-2010. Since then, the fresh fruit and vegetable indexes have exhibited volatile price movements with no real trend into 2012.

The price index for highly processed snacks (**Figure 17**) rose slowly in 2007, then accelerated upward during 2008 before falling back somewhat in 2009, then trending higher into 2012. The sugar and sweets price index had a similar pattern, although with a somewhat slower rise into 2012. The fats and oils price index showed more volatility rising rapidly through 2007 and the first nine months of 2008, then fell back through 2010 as the global market for oils became over-supplied, in part due to the fall-off in demand (related to the global financial crisis) in lesser-developed countries, where fats and oils are still treated as luxury goods. A resumption of global economic growth in late 2010 has pulled the fats and oils price index upward since early 2010, with a sharp uptick through 2011 before leveling off in 2012.

Figure 17. Monthly Retail Price Indexes: Sugar, Fat & Oils, and Snacks

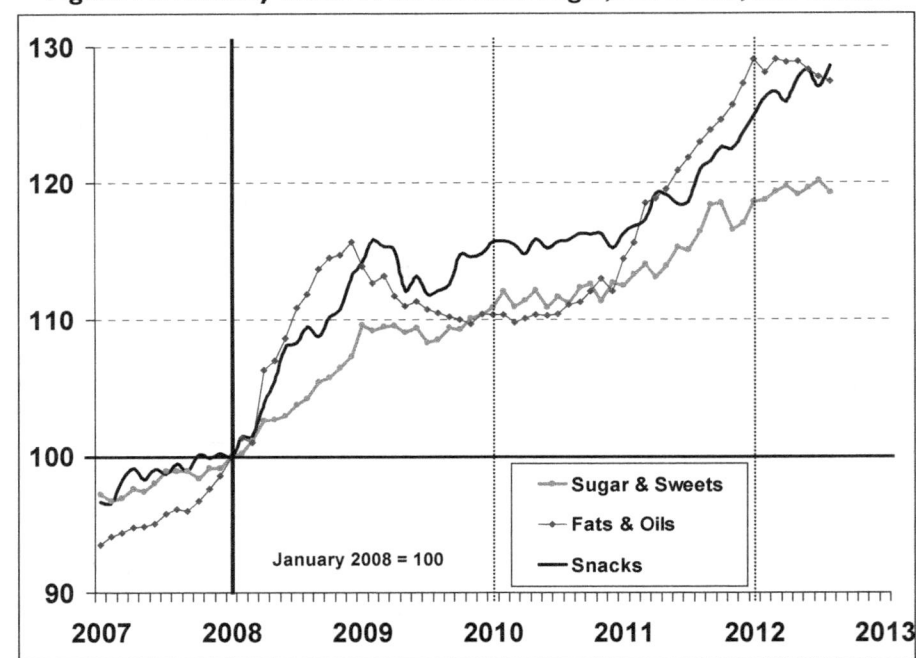

Source: Seasonally adjusted monthly CPI data, BLS, Department of Labor.

Similar to other highly processed food products, the prepared-food group (which includes frozen and freeze-dried prepared foods) and the carbonated beverages indexes tend to follow the swings in consumer demand as reflected by the general economy. Both indexes rose steadily through the first half of 2008 (**Figure 18**), then declined slightly into mid-2010 before ticking upward again with the global economic recovery. However, carbonated beverages have shown greater price inflation compared with prepared foods which are more dependent on the U.S. market. The slow U.S. economic recovery has kept prepared food demand in check. Coffee prices followed a similar, but more pronounced, pattern including a sharper rise in 2008, a more rapid descent through mid-2010 and very rapid price inflation until 2012 when prices declined sharply.

Figure 18. Monthly Retail Price Indexes: Coffee, Carbonated Beverages, and Prepared Foods

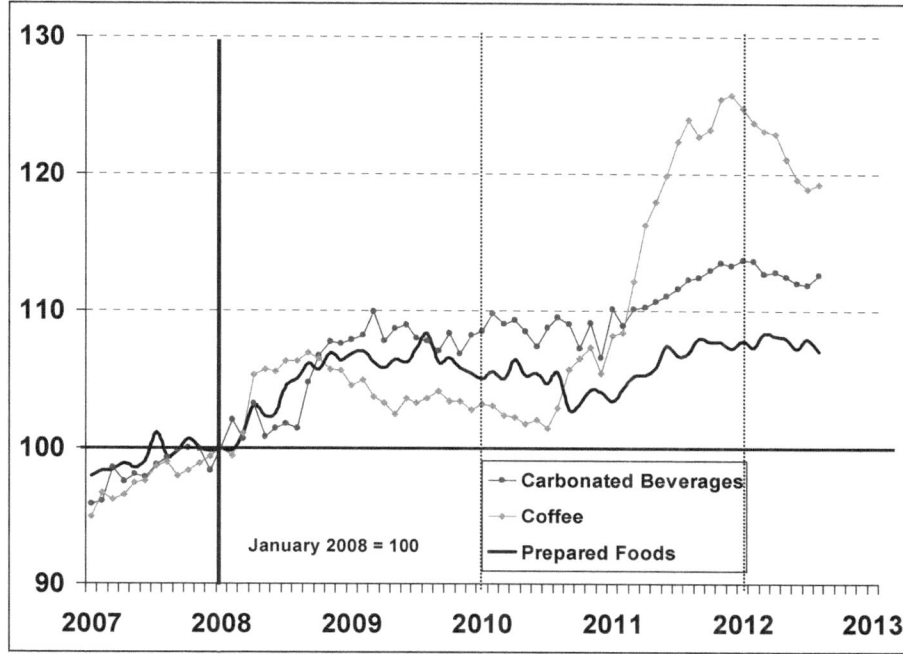

Source: Seasonally adjusted monthly CPI data, BLS, Department of Labor.

In sum, evidence from recent years suggests that highly processed foods more consistently adhere to steady, stable upward price trends dependent on general economic conditions. In contrast, prices for less-processed retail food products—such as eggs, milk, and fresh fruits and vegetables—respond far more quickly to changes in both farm commodity prices and economic conditions and have followed farm prices downward in the early months of 2009, then upward sharply from late 2010 into 2012 before leveling off or declining.

Effect of High Prices

For a given level of income, higher prices mean lower effective purchasing power, since the same household budget will now acquire a smaller volume of products. As stated earlier in this report, lower-income consumers who spend a significant share of their household budget on food are likely to be impacted more severely by rising food prices, to be more responsive to price changes, and to be forced to make more difficult budgetary tradeoffs than high-income consumers with lower food budget shares.

The surge in agricultural commodity prices as well as the rise in costs of raw materials, energy, and transportation that persisted from mid-2005 through early 2008 translated into higher retail prices for food and other household products with all-food CPI averaging 5.5% in 2008. The negative aspects of high retail prices was magnified by the global financial crisis that emerged in 2008. The economic downturn manifested itself in a decline in household wealth due to sharply lower real estate values, tighter business and consumer credit, and rising unemployment numbers.

Although commodity prices peaked in early 2008 and began a steady decline through 2010, most retail prices were slow to reflect wholesale commodity price declines, and it was only in early 2009 that retail prices significantly retreated for most foods. This price deflationary trend persisted into 2010 and provided some budgetary relief for households with employed members. However, surging unemployment numbers meant that many households were unable to take advantage of food price declines.

After a nearly two-year hiatus, commodity prices resumed their upward surge from mid-2010 into mid-2011 (**Figure 9**) before once again declining on economic weakness. As a result, food price inflation averaged 3.7% in 2011 and is projected to average in the 2.5% to 3.5% range in 2012 and slightly higher 3.0% to 4.0% in 2013 (**Figure 8**). The effect of higher food prices has been exacerbated by high U.S. unemployment rate associated with the economic recession of 2008 and 2009. The U.S. unemployment rate averaged 9.3% in 2009 and 9.6% in 2010 after averaging 5.0% during the previous decade (1999 to 2008). The unemployment rate has declined slowly to 9% in 2011 and is projected to fall to 8.2% in 2012, 8.0% in 2013, and 7.0% by 2015.[16]

Many wages and salaries, as well as federal programs (including several domestic food assistance programs), are linked to price inflation through escalation clauses in order to retain their purchasing power. For households where income does not keep up with price inflation, declines in purchasing power are both real and immediate. However, even for households with escalation clauses that adjust incomes or benefits for price inflation, there is a time lag between the time the price inflation is measured and the time when the wage or program benefit is adjusted upward to compensate. As a result, for households with incomes or federal benefits linked to price inflation escalators, higher prices can cause a short-term decline in real purchasing power. This is most meaningful when prices are accelerating. When prices are falling, as during a deflationary period, consumers with fixed incomes realize gains in real income (provided that they are not subject to wage cuts or layoffs).

Federal Spending for Domestic Food Assistance Programs[17]

The U.S. Department of Agriculture (USDA) administers several domestic food and nutrition programs that provide a nutritional safety net for millions of low-income households, as well as schoolchildren and nutritionally vulnerable groups such as pregnant and/or lactating mothers.[18] The past decade has seen a tremendous expansion in use of USDA's food and nutrition assistance programs—federal expenditures totaled $103.3 billion in FY2011 and marked the 11th consecutive year in which food and nutrition assistance expenditures exceeded the previous

---

[16] Global Insight, U.S. Flash Forecast, September 2012.

[17] For more information on the domestic food and nutrition programs discussed in this section, please contact Randy Alison Aussenberg, CRS Analyst in Social Policy (7-8641, raussenberg@crs.loc.gov).

[18] See CRS Report R42353, *Domestic Food Assistance: Summary of Programs*, by Randy Alison Aussenberg and Kirsten J. Colello.

historical record.[19] Since FY2000, expenditures for food and nutrition assistance have more than tripled.

The five largest food and nutrition assistance programs in FY2011 accounted for 96% of USDA's expenditures for food and nutrition assistance. Those programs are (1) the Supplemental Nutrition Assistance Program (SNAP), (2) the National School Lunch Program, (3) the Special Supplemental Nutrition Program for Women, Infants, and Children (WIC), (4) the Child and Adult Care Food Program, and (5) the School Breakfast Program. Each of these five major programs expanded, to varying degrees, during fiscal 2011.

A substantial portion of spending on these programs is in the form of entitlements (i.e., mandatory spending) whereby eligibility and participation rates govern outlays. For mandatory programs, food price inflation leads to more spending on domestic assistance efforts. Increasing prices encourage those who are eligible, but not participating, to enroll. They also translate directly (albeit with a time lag) into higher benefit payments and per-meal subsidies for "entitlement" programs in which benefits are indexed to food-price inflation. However, many of these programs also include discretionary components where outlays are determined through the annual appropriations process. Increasing prices place pressure on appropriators to provide more funding to support caseloads for "discretionary" programs like the WIC program.

The 2008-2009 global economic crisis—with its higher unemployment, income loss, and lower effective household purchasing power—following on the heels of higher retail prices, brought on higher participation rates and greater costs for domestic food aid programs. Although the U.S. economy resumed growth during 2010, unemployment ranks have been slow to follow. This is reflected in high SNAP participation levels, which hit an all-time high of 46.7 million (or 14.8% of the U.S. population) in June 2012 (the latest available information to date).[20] SNAP monthly benefit costs have grown from $2.8 billion in January 2008 to $6.2 billion in June 2012, with average per-person monthly benefit spending rising from $100 to $133.

Other domestic food assistance programs also have seen increased participation (and costs). The number of lower-income children receiving free or reduced-price school lunches has been consistently over 31 million schoolchildren since 2008.[21] Total outlays for the national school lunch, school breakfast, and special milk programs totaled $14.4 billion in FY2011.[22] WIC participation peaked at 9.2 million women, infants, and children in 2010,[23] while the total cost (food and administration) has crept upward to a high of $7.2 billion in FY2011.[24]

---

[19] *The Food Assistance Landscape*, FY2011 Annual Report, Economic Information Bulletin No. 93, March 2012, ERS, USDA, at http://www.ers.usda.gov/media/376910/eib93_1_.pdf.

[20] USDA, Food and Nutrition Service (FNS), Supplemental Nutrition Assistance Program, August 30, 2012, at http://www.fns.usda.gov/pd/snapmain.htm.

[21] USDA, FNS, Program Data—Child Nutrition Tables, August 30, 2012, at http://www.fns.usda.gov/pd/cnpmain.htm.

[22] USDA, FNS, Program Data—Child Nutrition Tables, "Federal Cost of School Food Programs," August 30, 2012, at http://www.fns.usda.gov/pd/cncosts.htm.

[23] USDA, FNS, WIC Program, "Monthly Data—National Level: October 2007–January 2011," at http://www.fns.usda.gov/pd/37WIC_Monthly.htm.

[24] USDA, FNS, WIC Program, "Annual Data—National Level: FY1974–FY2011," August 30, 2012, at http://www.fns.usda.gov/pd/wisummary.htm

Supplemental Nutrition Assistance Program (SNAP, formerly Food Stamps)

The SNAP, with nearly $75.7 billion in outlays in FY2011,[25] is the largest of the federally supported domestic food assistance programs.[26] SNAP benefits normally are indexed annually (each October) for changes in the cost of USDA's least costly food plan, the "Thrifty Food Plan" (TFP). For a number of years and well into 2006, annual increases in the cost of the TFP typically ranged between 1.5% and 2.5%. However, starting in late 2006, food prices reflected in the cost of items in the TFP began to increase at a much faster rate. For example, basic benefits were increased by 4.6% in FY2007 and by 8.5% in October 2008. While these were substantial increases, they lagged by three months in reflecting rising food costs—they were (by law) based on prices from the immediately previous June. Thus there is a three-month gap between the calculation of the price inflation index in June and its use to adjust SNAP benefits in October.

In recognition of the lag in the inflation index for SNAP benefits, increased food needs, and reduced income, the 2009 American Recovery and Reinvestment Act (ARRA; P.L. 111-5) provided additional support for domestic food assistance programs: an estimated $11.5 billion for FY2009-FY2010 and $20.8 billion through FY2019.[27] SNAP was the primary recipient of this new money, most of which will be used to pay for added benefits, loosened eligibility standards, and administrative costs.

However, these increased SNAP benefits were reduced as part of P.L. 111-226 (a law providing funding for education jobs and Medicaid) and were further reduced by child nutrition reauthorization legislation (the Healthy, Hunger-Free Kids Act of 2010; P.L. 111-296).[28] As a result of these cuts, in November 2013 SNAP benefits will revert to what basic SNAP law directs (i.e., as calculated using annual food-price inflation).

Child Nutrition

Federally supported child nutrition programs (e.g., the National School Lunch Program, the School Breakfast Program, the Special Milk Program, Child and Adult Care Food Program, and the Summer Food Service Program) and initiatives reach almost 32 million children. In FY2011, federal spending on these programs totaled nearly $17.5 billion, the second-largest federal commitment to domestic food assistance.[29] The basic goals of federal child nutrition programs are to improve children's nutrition, increase lower-income children's access to nutritious meals and snacks, and help support the agricultural economy.

---

[25] USDA, FNS, Supplemental Nutrition Assistance Program, "National Level: Annual Summary, FY69 through FY2010," at http://www.fns.usda.gov/pd/SNAPsummary.htm.

[26] See CRS Report R42505, *Supplemental Nutrition Assistance Program (SNAP): A Primer on Eligibility and Benefits*, by Randy Alison Aussenberg.

[27] For more information, see CRS Report R40160, *Agriculture, Nutrition, and Rural Provisions in the American Recovery and Reinvestment Act (ARRA) of 2009*, coordinated by Jim Monke.

[28] For more information see CRS Report R41374, *Reducing SNAP (Food Stamp) Benefits Provided by the ARRA: P.L. 111-226 and P.L. 111-296*, by Randy Alison Aussenberg, Jim Monke, and Gene Falk.

[29] USDA, FNS, Program Data—Child Nutrition Tables, at http://www.fns.usda.gov/pd/cnpmain.htm.

Federal payments for meals and snacks served to children are indexed every July to food-price changes reflected in the food-away-from-home component of the CPI over the 12-month period ending each May. Commodity support (some 23 cents per meal in 2011) also is indexed annually based on the Bureau of Labor Statistics' Producer Price Index for five major food components (cereal and bakery products, meats, poultry and fish, dairy products, processed fruits and vegetables, and fats and oils).

On December 13, 2010, Congress enacted the most sweeping changes in child nutrition and WIC programs since the 1970s.[30] The Healthy, Hunger-Free Kids Act of 2010 (P.L. 111-296) made substantial changes in child nutrition and WIC programs (most importantly, increasing federal financing for school lunches) that were estimated to cost just about $4.5 billion over 10 years. However, the act included spending reductions achieved by reducing future benefits under SNAP to offset the act's costs, and dropped authority for the Agriculture Department to bar certain foods from the WIC program.

The WIC Program

Unlike the SNAP and child nutrition programs, which receive mandatory funding, the WIC program is funded from discretionary sources. Spending depends on annual appropriations, based largely on estimates of participation and the cost of the food packages that are purchased with WIC vouchers. In FY2011, $7.2 billion was spent on WIC including $5 billion in food costs and $2 billion in nutrition service and administrative costs.[31] The average monthly food cost per participant was $46.67.

The value of benefits is not indexed, per se. Rather, WIC vouchers are redeemable at whatever the participating retailer charges for the items covered by the vouchers, which differ according to the type of recipient (e.g., pregnant mother, infant, child). As a result, the cost of WIC vouchers reflect food price changes without the time lag built into other inflation-indexed nutrition programs. Just as important, WIC vouchers are highly specific as to the food items they cover and have a relatively heavy emphasis on certain types of food—for example, dairy items and infant formula are major components.

In recent years, the cost of WIC food vouchers has varied a great deal, largely because of changes in dairy-related food prices. The average per-participant monthly cost of vouchers has ranged from $33.06 in FY2000 to $46.67 in FY2011. However, the annual percentage increase has actually declined in some years (FY2005 and FY2006) and increased substantially in other years (6.6% for FY2004, 5.3% for FY2007, and 12.6% in 2011). Given this significant volatility, it is difficult to produce specific estimates of the effect of food price inflation on WIC program costs.

Although WIC spending is discretionary, Congress has historically shown a willingness to appropriate whatever amounts are necessary to meet costs imposed by increased participation or food costs. In 2009, it provided a $400 million contingency reserve to meet unexpected costs in FY2009 and FY2010 as part of the ARRA. In FY2010, $7,252 million was appropriated for WIC.

---

[30] See CRS Report R41354, *Child Nutrition and WIC Reauthorization: P.L. 111-296*, by Randy Alison Aussenberg.

[31] USDA, FNS, WIC Program Data at: http://www.fns.usda.gov/pd/wicmain.htm.

However, budget appropriations included cuts in discretionary WIC spending of 7.1% to $6,734 million for FY2011 and another 1.7% to $6,618.5 million for FY2012, respectively.[32]

Additional Commodity Assistance Programs

USDA operates several additional food assistance programs targeting low-income or vulnerable populations. The Emergency Food Assistance Program (TEFAP) and meal service programs under the Older Americans Act (e.g., "meals-on-wheels" and meals served to seniors in congregate meal settings) provide key food assistance support for vulnerable groups. The Commodity Supplemental Food Program (CSFP) provides foods purchased by USDA to low-income infants and children up to age six, low-income pregnant and postpartum women, and to low-income seniors citizens. The Senior Farmers' Market Nutrition Program (SFMNP) provides coupons to low-income seniors that can be exchanged for fresh, nutritious, unprepared, locally-grown fruits, vegetables, and herbs at farmers' markets, roadside stands, and community-supported agriculture programs. Like the WIC program, these programs are discretionary, and rising need and higher food prices have placed pressure on appropriators to add to federal funding. In FY2012, $242.3 million was appropriated for these programs.[33]

Foreign Food Aid

USDA's international activities are funded by discretionary appropriations (e.g., foreign food assistance under the Food for Peace Act (P.L. 480) and by using the borrowing authority of the CCC (e.g., export credit guarantees, market development programs, and export subsidies).[34] Because foreign food aid is a budget value and not a food volume, its effective "purchase power" is diminished by food price hikes without additional appropriations. Unlike some domestic nutrition programs, foreign food aid is not adjusted to account for changing costs.

Food aid usually takes the form of basic food grains such as wheat, sorghum, and corn, and vegetable oil—commodities critical to developing-country diets. Since there is very little value added for these commodities, shifts in prices translate directly into higher prices for food-insecure countries or reduced food aid contributions per dollar spent. Also, higher energy costs have increased shipping costs for both food purchases and food aid.

---

[32] See CRS Report R42596, *Agriculture and Related Agencies: FY2013 Appropriations*, by Jim Monke.

[33] USDA, *FY2012 Budget, Explanatory Notes for Committee on Appropriation, Volume 2*, February 2011.

[34] For more information, see CRS Report R41072, *International Food Aid Programs: Background and Issues*, by Charles E. Hanrahan.

Author Contact Information

Randy Schnepf
Specialist in Agricultural Policy
rschnepf@crs.loc.gov, 7-4277

www.ingramcontent.com/pod-product-compliance
Lightning Source LLC
Chambersburg PA
CBHW080640290526
45790CB00007B/3147